You Play
Pop Songs
Collection for Young Voices

With Parts for Keyboard, Guitar and Classroom Instruments
Arranged by Tom Anderson

T0056508

ISBN 978-1-4584-2085-5

HAL•LEONARD®
CORPORATION
7777 W. BLUEMOUND RD. P.O. BOX 13819 MILWAUKEE, WI 53213

Visit Hal Leonard Online at
www.halleonard.com

Fireflies

About the Song

"Fireflies" was a #1 hit in 2009 for Owl City. Owl City is a recording project by singer/songwriter Adam Young that began in his parents' basement in Minnesota. His music spread initially through social networking.

Instrumental Accompaniment Parts

KEYBOARD & GUITAR

Keyboard (KB) and Guitar may be used to accompany this song. They do not always play at the same time. Their entrances are indicated in the music. Guitarists will strum either quarter notes or half notes as marked in the music.

Here are four basic accompaniment rhythms for the keyboard. The first rhythm shows the piano playing chord arpeggios (broken chords) in the right hand and quarter notes in the left. Make sure to change chords where the chord symbols appear. One student may play the chords in the top staff, as another plays the bass part in the lower staff.

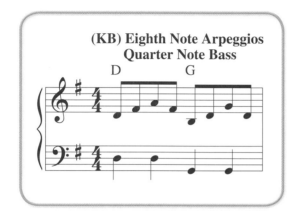

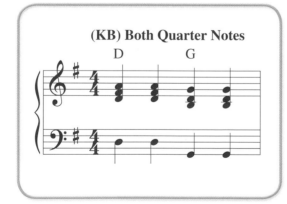

The chord progression includes chords where the root is not the lowest note. This type of chord is called a *slash chord*. The chord appears to the left of the slash and the bass note to the right in the chord symbol.

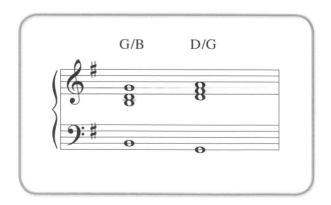

PERCUSSION PARTS

Here are optional percussion parts. The Triangle is to be played using an open tone (o) where it is allowed to ring and closed tone (+) where it is muffled by holding it with two fingers.

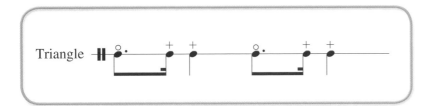

Shakers are played using sixteenth notes. Make sure the beads strike the edges rhythmically by moving the hand crisply and slightly accenting the first sixteenth note in each beat.

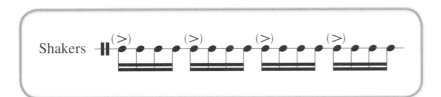

The Drum is played using three different tones: low, high and slap. The low tone is played in the middle of the drum. The high tone is played at the edge. A slap is produced by cupping the left hand towards the edge of the drum while resting it on the drumhead. Strike the edge of the drum with the right hand as if slapping it. Practice this rhythm slowly before attempting it up to tempo.

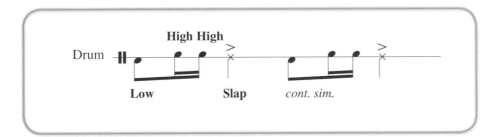

The percussion entrances are cued in Teacher Part. They are played during the Verse and Chorus.

PITCHED INSTRUMENTS

Separate music parts for Soprano Glockenspiel, Soprano, Alto and Bass Metallophones are included in the Student Part. Their entrances are cued in the Teacher Part.

Recorded by OWL CITY

Fireflies

Words and Music by ADAM YOUNG
Arranged by TOM ANDERSON

Moderate with underlying groove (♩ = 90)

Firework

About the Song

"Firework" was a #1 hit for singer Katy Perry in 2010. Its lyrics speak of being the best person possible so that others see your potential.

Instrumental Accompaniment Parts

KEYBOARD & GUITAR

Keyboard (KB) and Guitar may be used to accompany "Firework." The keyboard plays throughout the song. Here are samples of the quarter note and eighth note rhythms as suggested in the Student Part. One student may play the chords on a piano or keyboard as another plays the bass part in the lower portion. Guitarists will strum quarter notes, and play only during certain sections, as marked in the music.

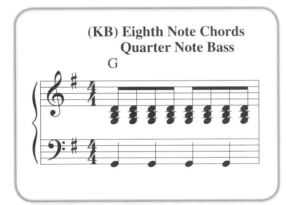

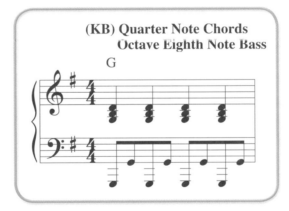

PERCUSSION PARTS

Here are optional percussion parts. One set of rhythms is played during the Verse and the second is played during the Chorus, Interlude and Coda. Do not play these instruments during the Pre Chorus.

PITCHED INSTRUMENTS

Xylophones may be added during the Verse. This part should be played with rhythmic precision at a medium loud volume level.

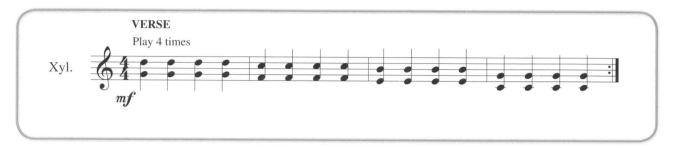

Do not play the Xylophones during the Pre Chorus. Add this new part to the Chorus and the Coda at a loud volume. The mallet pattern of L-R-L (cross over)-R may be used.

Metallophones or any other pitched instrument that rings may be played during the Interlude. Allow the instruments to ring freely.

Recorded by KATY PERRY

Firework

Words and Music by MIKKEL ERIKSEN,
TOR ERIK HERMANSEN, ESTHER DEAN,
KATY PERRY and SANDY WILHELM
Arranged by TOM ANDERSON

al - read - y bur - ied deep, six feet un - der screams, but no one seems to hear a thing?
all the doors are closed so you could o - pen one that leads you to the per - fect road.

Do you know that there's still a chance for you? 'Cause there's a spark in you.
Like a light - ning bolt, your heart will glow; and when it's time we know.

21 PRE CHORUS

You just got - ta ig - nite the light and let it shine.

Guitar out
End Xyl.&Perc.

Just own the night like the Fourth of Ju - ly.

Hey, Soul Sister

About the Song

"Hey, Soul Sister" was a Top 10 hit for the band, Train. It was the first single from their fifth studio album, *Save Me, San Francisco*. The lead guitarist had to learn to play ukulele to play the song. Its sound is an integral part of the accompaniment.

Instrumental Accompaniment Parts

KEYBOARD & GUITAR

Keyboard (KB) and Guitar may be used to accompany this song. They do not always play at the same time. Their entrances are indicated in the music.

The Guitar part features partial and full chords. The partial chords emulate the sound of a ukulele. Here is one possible rhythm to play during the Intro. The sixteenth notes should be swung slightly where they are played unevenly (long-short-long-short).

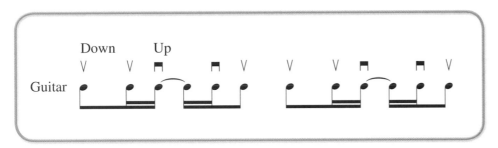

When the Keyboard part enters at M. 13, it uses whole note chords. At M. 21, the Keyboard part uses a *reggae rhythm*. Half notes are played in the bass while the right hand plays on the *off beats* (the "and" of the beat) alternating between sixteenth and eighth notes.

PERCUSSION PARTS

Here are optional percussion parts. The Shaker part alternates between eighth note and sixteenth note rhythms. Again, the off beat is an important part of the rhythm. It is played as an eighth note rhythm and also accented in a sixteenth note rhythm.

The Bass Drum plays this rhythm for most of the song. Listen to the original Train recording as an example. It was played on the Bass Drum of the drum set.

 NOTE: This rhythm is played on the Bass Drum except for the pickup to m. 41 where quarter notes are played on beats 3 and 4.

The Tambourine is played on beats 2 and 4; the *back beat*. This is one of the simplest forms of syncopation.

The percussion entrances are cued in the Teacher Part.

 **PITCHED INSTRUMENTS**

Separate music parts for Soprano, Alto and Bass Metallophones are included in the Student Part. Their entrances are cued in the Teacher Part.

Recorded by TRAIN

Hey, Soul Sister

Words and Music by PAT MONAHAN,
ESPEN LIND and AMUND BJORKLAND
Arranged by TOM ANDERSON

24

Viva La Vida

About the Song

"Viva La Vida" was a #1 hit in 2008 for the English rock band, Coldplay. It was the first #1 hit for them in the United States and United Kingdom. It won a Grammy Award as Song of the Year in 2009. The title is Spanish for "long live life."

Instrumental Accompaniment Parts

KEYBOARD & GUITAR

Keyboard (KB) and Guitar may be used to accompany this song. The repetitive, four-measure accompaniment figure can be played by both KB and Gtr.

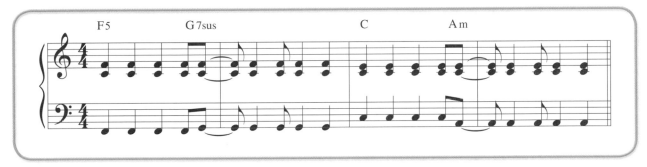

It does not change until the Coda at M. 117 when whole notes are played.

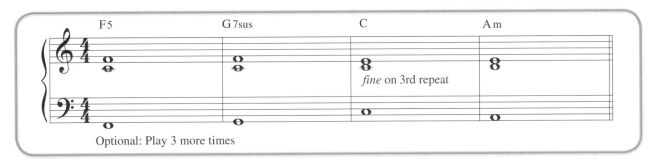

Orff instruments may be played in the last eleven measures. If they are not available, Keyboards may play this part. The final chord to be played is C major.

PERCUSSION PARTS

Here are optional percussion parts. The Bass Drum enters at M. 9. Steady quarter notes are played until M. 117.

Suspended Cymbal and Timpani (optional Tom Toms) roll their notes and then let them ring. They begin at M. 41. Their entrances are cued in the Teacher Part.

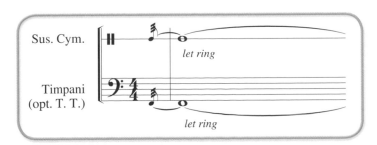

PITCHED INSTRUMENTS

Soprano, Alto and Bass Xylophones play the main accompaniment rhythm beginning at M. 5. This part is played until M. 117.

An optional Contrabass Bars part begins at M. 41. Its entrances are cued in the Teacher Part.

The Alto and Bass Metallophones play octave C's in MM. 41 – 56 and 81 – 116.

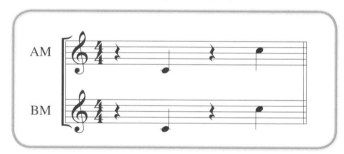

A whole-note rhythm is played in MM. 73 – 80 and 121 – 131.

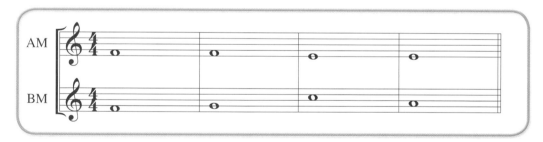

It is played twice the first time and three times in MM. 121 – 131. Only the first three measures are played on the third repeat. The Soprano Metallophone is played in MM. 57 – 64 using an eighth-note rhythm. These four measures are played twice.

Whole notes are played in MM. 73 – 80 and MM. 121 – 131.

The Recorder part is cued in the Teacher Part.

Recorded by COLDPLAY

Viva La Vida

Words and Music by GUY BERRYMAN, JON BUCKLAND,
WILL CHAMPION and CHRIS MARTIN
Arranged by TOM ANDERSON

Waka Waka (This Time for Africa)

About the Song

"Waka Waka (This Time for Africa)" was a Top-40 hit for Shakira in 2010. It was the official song for the 2010 FIFA World Cup. She performed the song at the opening ceremonies with the African fusion band, Freshlyground.

Instrumental Accompaniment Parts

KEYBOARD & GUITAR

Keyboard (KB) and Guitar may be used to accompany this song. They both start at M. 9 and play the same rhythms throughout the song, as marked in the Teacher and Student parts.

Here are the three basic rhythms played by the keyboard and guitar.

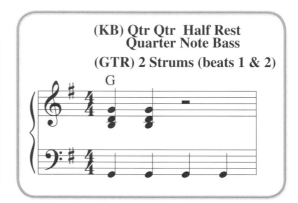

PERCUSSION PARTS

Here are optional percussion parts. The Shekere, Djembe and Bass Drum are the percussion instruments played in the sections designated as Partial Percussion.

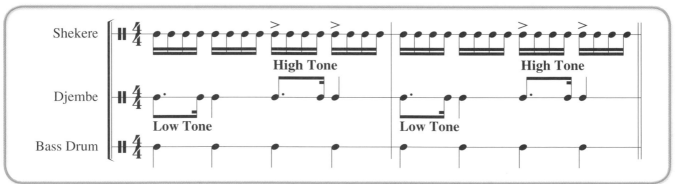

Two tones are played on the Djembe. The *low tone* is played in the middle of the drum. It can be played using a closed fist and striking the drum with the side of the hand. The *high tone* is played at the edge of the drum using the fleshy part of the fingers.

The Triangle and Shakers are added to the Full Percussion sections.

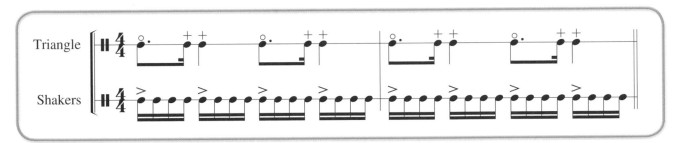

The Triangle is to be played using an open tone (o) where it is allowed to ring and closed tone (+) where it is muffled by holding it with two fingers.

PITCHED INSTRUMENTS

Soprano, Alto and Bass Xylophones begin at M. 5 and are played throughout. This rhythm is played most of the time.

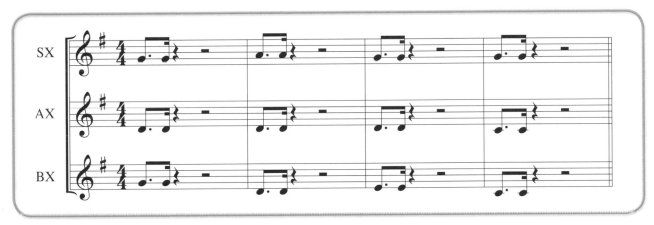

A quarter note is played on beat 1 whenever the rhythm section stops on that beat. This rhythm is cued in the Student Part.

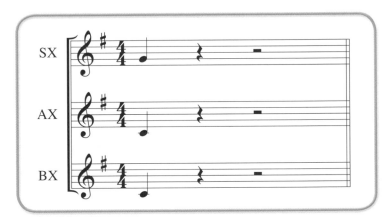

OPTIONAL IMPROVISATION

An improvised solo may be played in MM. 29 – 36 and 85 – 91. It can be played on any pitched instrument using these notes. This is a *pentatonic scale* that matches the chord progression. Use various patterns of pitches and rhythms in the improvised solo.

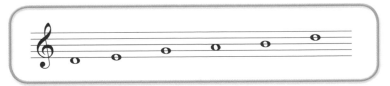

Recorded by SHAKIRA

Waka Waka
(This Time for Africa)

Words and Music by SHAKIRA, ZOLANI MAHOLA,
JOHN HILL, DOOH BELLY EUGENE VICTOR,
ZE BELL JEAN PAUL and EMILE KOJIDIE
Arranged by TOM ANDERSON